BRENDAN LANDY

GABRIEL FITZMAURICE

THE FATHER'S PART

THE FATHER'S PART

POEMS BY GABRIEL FITZMAURICE

STORY LINE PRESS
1992

First American Printing

This publication was made possible thanks to the generous support of the Nicholas Roerich Museum, and the Andrew W. Mellon Foundation.

ISBN: 0-934257-

Book design by Lysa McDowell

Published by Story Line Press, Inc.
Three Oaks Farm in Brownsville, OR 97327

ACKNOWLEDGMENTS

Grateful acknowledgment is made to the editors of the following publications where several of these poems first appeared:

Ballyguiltenane Rural Journal
Europa (Leuven, Belgium)
The Great Book of Ireland
Poetry Ireland Review
Radio Kerry (*The Rambling House, Saturday Review*)
RTE Radio I (*The Poet's Voice, The Sunday Show*)
The Salmon (Galway)
Stet (Cork)
Writing in the West (Galway)

OTHER BOOKS BY
GABRIEL FITZMAURICE

Poetry in English

Rainsong (Beaver Row Press, Dublin 1984)
Road to the Horizon (Beaver Row Press, Dublin 1987)
Dancing Through (Beaver Row Press, Dublin 1990)

Poetry in Irish

Nocht (Coiscéim, Dublin 1989)

Children's Poetry

The Moving Stair (The Kerryman, Tralee 1989)

Translation

The Purge (Beaver Row Press, Dublin 1989)

Editor

The Flowering Tree/An Crann Faoi Bhláth
(With Declan Kiberd), Wolfhound Press, Dublin 1991.
Between the Hills and Sea: Songs and Ballads of Kerry
(Oidhreacht, Ballyheigue 1991.)
Con Greaney: Traditional Singer (Oidhreacht, Ballyheighe 1991.)

CONTENTS

For John
with love.

UPON MY WORD

Safe and snug and somnolent
As any half-dead thing,
Cocooned in transformation
I wake up to my Spring.

The laser light unclouds my eyes,
My vision is restored
Original as Eden.
Upon every word

Depends this whole creation
Where a thing beocmes its name
As Adam creates his paradise—
Every word a frame.

THE FATHER'S PART

No more am I just teacher—
In any case, you learn:

Water's wet,
A bottle's good,
If you touch fire, you burn.

So much you learn without me;
I have so much to learn
In this wordless world.

Though you're not flesh of my sperm,
The paternal lights within me
And the thorns round my heart
Are scorched like scrub from bogland...

Mine
Is the father's part.

"Son"
I call you
And the name possesses:

What the Board made legal,
The word makes true.

Your first "da-da".
My first "son"
Have named our recognition.

Later
You may venture on your own
Seeking
What even this love can't give.

No matter:

We inhabit our appellations,
"Daddy"
"Son",
Part of each other's language...

This will live.

BEDTIME

You prance about your cot,
Refuse to sleep.

I can't command you
Who have no words.

Defeated,
I take you to my bed
And lie beside you.

You tug my hair,
Gouge my eyes,
Babble,
Kick.

If you had words
You wouldn't be so spoiled—

Unbroken
On the bit of language
Yet, sweet child.

PHOTOGRAPH

Your image in the viewfinder
Says so much more than "cheese":

My son, It names you perfectly—
"John",
"Bright eyes",
"Sweet breath",
I interpret.

You are all demand—
Your every whim is humoured;
Your cry is my command.

You taste the world in mouthfuls
Till every common noun
Is seasoned by its adjective...

I press the sensor down.

PRESENTATION

On Christmas Eve
We present our child
(Adopted all these years)
First
In the ancestral home.

Tom, paterfamilias,
Kisses him.

This is the floor
Tom's father crawled,
My father crawled.

Mary,
Woman of the house,
Coaxes him across the floor.

Now
You're a Fitzmaurice

And in this ancestral home
With cousins,
Aunts and uncles
You are welcome;

For you're our new communion—
The family receive
As Mary pours a health to you
On this first Christmas Eve.

John
You have achieved a tooth—

Painfully it came
Latent
Through your gum,
A pinnacle of perseverance.

If what must will come,
It's well that we have Calpol...

The baby sucks his thumb.

MAGIC

You press the shaft—
You get a sound:

The bell rings
And the horses dance
On your miniature merry-go-round.

What are horses?

You dunno—
But *Dug-et! Dug-et!*
You can't make 'em go.

Elow-el!
Yes I'm looking—

You've never done this before.

Again
You work your magic—

Then chuck it on the floor.

This is the first constriction
Fitted to your feet—

Later
There will be other constrictions
Equally for your benefit.

Learn to walk—

In winter
Shod;

In summer
Barefoot
Feel the road;

Splash through water,
Squelch through mud—

Let your toes decide what's good.

Though the mind
In terror balk,
The feet are constant...

Courage! Walk!

JOHN PLAYING AMONG PANSIES

You ignore the pansies.

Not now content to crawl,
One day you'll see their beauty...

No art before a fall.

He knocks the shampoo in the bath—
His look asks
"Is this wrong or right?"

I commend his naive act.

Puzzled by his action
My son makes God of me,
Remains a child in Eden
Till he eats of every tree.

Adam was right to eat the apple—

He was utterly unfree,
Kept,
A child in Eden.

He'd have left the garden anyway
With his wife and kids
Moral only in his freedom.

I slice an apple for my son,
Give it him to eat;

He bites it,
The grimaces—

Finds it sour
But sweet.

Who could swim,
I believe, at birth
Have forgotten how to swim....

Water of our origin
Shocks you to a grin—
Sans gill
Sans tail
Sans fin
You stiffen with excitement,
Tug me to come in.

Water of the spirit, this,
Water of the fin—
Water undivided.

Immersed in this holy water,
Revelling in his role,
A father voices-forth
Fulfilled—

His son has made him whole.

Whatever I believe in,
I believe in this—
The Easter sung
As I make soup,
Break bread for you,
My son.

While I ponder my belief
(In Easter or in art?)
Off you toddle with the trust—
The blessing of a laugh...

Like any Dad, I kiss you,
Give you bread for crust.

You don't know yet
What a kiss is...

Eat my love in trust.

CHRIST THE SAVIOUR

Yes!
I'll translate you Christ the Saviour—
In doubt,
In death,
The bulb of Easter.

Ever man interprets myth—
Manifests himself.

So I begin with hope and glory—
Life alone reveals the story.

"ADOPTED"

I interpolate "adopted"
In baby-talk with you
In hopes that when you're verbal
It won't hurt you.

As you grow up into language
You'll flower through many names—
Sprout then through "adopted"...

In time, son, I'll explain.

Five seasons into language
And Babel's not the same
Pronouncing "Mama", "Dada",
You recognize your name.

Babbling to your Pentecost,
You hear and understand—
The first sign is obedience:
Clap handies, John! Clap hands!

You hear
—Not words
But rhyming sounds
And you obey the rhyme,
Clap handies to my "sandy"
As I learned at the beach...

Here
Language is a symphony
Where you pick up the rhyme,
Where things are sounds
And names are sung
And nothing is defined.

"NO"

The first real word you uttered, son,
Was "no"—

First song of the ego,
It defines you...

When "yes" affirms nothing
But fear and public show
What sings,
Joins hands,
Lights candles?

This democratic "no".

You mark yourself by accident,
Chuckle, mark again
Till, banded like a mackerel,
You chew upon the pen.

I wrench the marker from your fist,
Scrub shin and knee and thigh,
Your tugs and twists accuse me...
Who saw the fish but I?

TANNY

We have created Santa Claus
(An image of our love)—
Mostly unspectacular,
The man I'm thinking of.

And you have grown towards Tanny
Allowing love to be
Familiar in his image;
You lisp his name with glee.

Yes! I believe in Santa
Whom others might call God-
But Santa changes nappies...
No! Tanny's not a cod.

WHAT'S IN A NAME?
OR THE IMPORTANCE OF BEING JOHN

Mairéad you call him
Whose name is *John*—
No matter that Mairéad's his sister.

Mairéad you call him
For you are John
And there can't be two of one.

So what if there are two *Mairéads*—
Mairéad's a name
(Your JOHN is not)
And it's all the same
What name he's got.

Besides

You like Mairéad—
She plays with you:

It's really an accolade
To be called *Mairéad* !

Come on!
His name is *John*.

But this is no game you're playing at—

Mairéad's his name:
Maw-rade ! That's that.

ART

You sprawl on the floor
Scribbling on an invoice
Ignoring *Tom and Jerry* on T.V.

"I make it! I write the picture!"
You divert me, imploring
"That's John's picture."

I let you be.

Then
"Up Daybo's lap!"
You dance and tug me.

"No John!
Daybo's writing poems"—

A pause...

"John write a pone! John write a pone!"
You barter.

Your ploy shines on refusal
And it thaws.

Sitting on my lap,
You grab my biro,
Cover Daybo's draft about you
With your scrawl—

"That's Daybo's pone", you beam,
"Dirty! Dirty!"

Inherent in creation is its fall.

You seem fonder of Granda than of me;
But then, you need me more—

This is the need that causes sons
To close the door on Daddy.

If that day comes
(For adventure will be free)
I give you all a father can—
A welcome and a key.

Returning to my father,
I offer all I grew...

You have won your way to Granda's plate—
We're one again through you.

The old man in the Bank who knew my mother
Examines you, and, with myopic eye,
Pronounces your resemblance. You're related...
"He has the brown head of the Cunninghams", I reply!

YOUR NAME

She took my name,
Adopted it
That two might grow as one;

We budded, blossomed;
That we might fruit
Adopted you, my son.

You are our forbidden fruit—
By desire and name
One of us, now family...

Your name, son—
Say your name.

Grafted to your parents,
You have taken and grow strong.
A robin twitters from this bush...
O joy (and threat) of song.

AND THE WORD WAS MADE FLESH...

All my life I knew its lack
—That which had no name-
Though its light shone in the darkness.

I called it many names,
But my heart was ever restless
Until you came to my vocab.
In a Babygro of blue—

You're my word incarnate...
I lay my head on you.

AN ONLY CHILD NO LONGER

John, tomorrow you'll have a sister—
How's that going to affect you? And me?
Your Daybo'll become "da-da" to his daughter
And I'll be no longer yours exclusively.

John, forgive me this betrayal—
Though we've drawn "John's baby", I fear you'll see it thus
When Nessa cries and captures all attention
And you hide your face prostrate in a fuss.

Tonight you're monarch of your kingdom
Where everything is "John's" that you can grab.
Tomorrow you must share, and I must teach you
Who healed me with your childhood and your gab.

NOTES FOR AMERICAN READERS:

In the poem *Song for a New Tooth*, "Calpol" is an infant pain-reliever.

In the poem *And the Word Was Made Flesh...*, a "Babygro" is an infant stretch-suit.

BIOGRAPHICAL NOTE:

Gabriel Fitzmaurice was born, in 1952, in Moyvane, Co. Kerry, where he lives and teaches in the local Primary School.

Chairman and Literary Advisor of Writers' Week, Listowel, he has published collections of poetry in English and Irish. He has also published a collection of children's verse.

He has edited, with Declan Kiberd, a major anthology of contemporary verse in Irish, with verse translations. His translations from the Irish have been widely published.

Formerly a Contributing Editor to 2 PLUS 2, the international literary magazine from Lausanne, Switzerland, in 1987 he represented Ireland at Europees Poeziefestival, the European Festival of Poetry in Louvain, Belgium. He is currently the Irish correspondent of the European Society for the Promotion of Poetry whose headquarters are in Louvain.

His poetry has been translated into French and Dutch. An award winner at the Gerard Manly Hopkins Centenary Poetry Competition, he has broadcast extensively on Irish radio and television. He has played on two albums of traditional Irish music and has produced and sung on a compilation album of the songs and ballads of Kerry.